ADVENTURES IN SPACE

CHRIS HADFIELD
AND THE INTERNATIONAL SPACE STATION

Andrew Langley

raintree

a Capstone company — publishers for children

Raintree is an imprint of Capstone Global Library Limited, a company incorporated in England and Wales having its registered office at 7 Pilgrim Street, London, EC4V 6LB – Registered company number: 6695582

www.raintree.co.uk
myorders@raintree.co.uk

Edited by Clare Lewis and Abby Colich
Designed by Steve Mead and Justin Hoffman
Original illustrations © Capstone Global Library Ltd 2015
Illustrated by Justin Hoffman
Picture research by Svetlana Zhurkin
Production by Victoria Fitzgerald
Originated by Capstone Global Library Ltd
Printed and bound in China

ISBN 978 1 406 29741 6
19 18 17 16 15
10 9 8 7 6 5 4 3 2 1

British Library Cataloguing in Publication Data
A full catalogue record for this book is available from the British Library.

Acknowledgements
We would like to thank the following for permission to reproduce photographs:
AP Images: Rex Features, 30; NASA, cover, 4, 5, 6, 8, 9, 10, 11, 12, 13, 17, 20, 21, 22, 23, 24, 25, 26, 27, 28, 31, 32—33, 35, 37, Carla Cioffi, 38, 39, JPL/Cornell University, 40, Victor Zelentsov, 19; Newscom: EPA/Maxim Shipenkov, 18, EPA/Stephanie Pilick, 42, ITAR-TASS, 7

We would like to thank Dr Geza Gyuk for his invaluable help in the preparation of this book.

CONTENTS

All words in bold, **like this**, appear in the glossary on page 45.

FIRE ALARM!

Chris Hadfield was fast asleep. He was aboard the International Space Station (ISS), flying about 400 kilometres (250 miles) above Earth. Suddenly, a horn was blaring. Hadfield was awake in an instant, and so were his three US crewmates. They looked at the emergency lights on the wall to see what was wrong. It was the fire alarm!

DEALING WITH DANGER

Fire is one of the biggest threats on any spacecraft. It can cause massive damage and fast. You can't escape because there's nowhere to go. **Astronauts** are trained not to panic, but to solve the problem carefully and calmly.

◼ **Chris Hadfield and his crew made regular checks of the complex equipment aboard the ISS.**

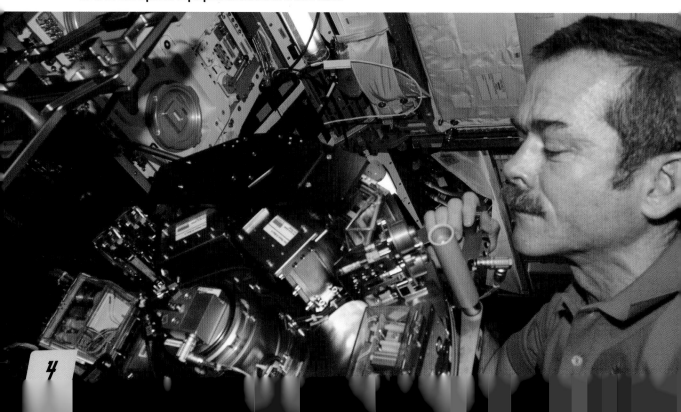

One of Hadfield's men alerted the Russian crew members, who slept in a different part of the ISS. Together, they checked the computer systems and **smoke detectors**. There was no sign of fire. They decided the alarm was triggered by an electrical fault, and went back to bed.

What is the International Space Station?

The International Space Station (ISS) is a flying **research laboratory** that **orbits** Earth. Developed by the United States, Russia, Japan, Europe and Canada, it is home to a crew of up to six astronauts, who conduct scientific experiments while on board. The ISS is constructed of several pieces that were launched separately, starting in 1998, and assembled in space.

LIVING IN SPACE

Chris Hadfield had faced many potentially dangerous moments like this one. He'd already flown on two missions into space. Now, in 2013 and on his third space trip, he was commander of the ISS. Altogether, he would spend 165 days (more than five months) in space during his career, and he would travel 113.2 million kilometres (70 million miles). This made him one of the most experienced space travellers of all time.

BECOMING AN ASTRONAUT

Chris Hadfield's life changed forever on 20 July 1969. That evening, he watched live TV footage as Neil Armstrong climbed out of his spacecraft and became the first person to step on to the Moon. Chris was just nine years old, but he was already certain of one thing: he wanted to be an astronaut.

■ Edwin "Buzz" Aldrin was the second human to step on to the Moon from *Apollo 11* in 1969. The first to land was Neil Armstrong, who took this picture.

INTO THE AIR

There was one big problem. The US space programme was run by the National Aeronautics and Space Administration (NASA). Back then, NASA only accepted US citizens for astronaut training. Chris Hadfield is a Canadian.

Not wanting to give up so soon, Hadfield did the next best thing. He joined the Air Force division of the Canadian Armed Forces. At training school he was named Top Pilot of 1980 and top graduate in 1983. In 1988, he went on to become a **test pilot** in the United States, flying new types of aircraft and engines. This was very dangerous work, but he showed he had exceptional skills in the air.

ASTRONAUT AT LAST

Hadfield's big break came in 1992. The Canadian Space Agency announced it was hiring astronauts, who would train with NASA. He applied right away – but there were 5,329 other **applicants**. After many weeks of interviews, Chris was told he was one of only four candidates to be selected.

■ **Yuri Gagarin was the first person in space.**

The space pioneers

First **satellite** sending signals from space: *Sputnik* (Russia), October 1957

First human in space: Yuri Gagarin (Russia), April 1961

First American in space: Alan Shepard, May 1961

First woman in space: Valentina Tereshkova (Russia), June 1963

First human on the Moon: Neil Armstrong (USA), July 1969

IN THE CLASSROOM

No one walks into NASA and expects to go straight into space. First, there are many years of hard training in order to learn how to operate the most complicated machines ever built. Then there is the simple fact that many astronauts never go into space at all. Opportunities are very limited.

■ **Chris Hadfield (back row, third from right) was one of the first two Canadian pilots to join astronaut training at NASA.**

Chris Hadfield began his training at the NASA Space Center in Texas, USA, in August 1992. He found it a lot like going to school. The trainees spent long hours studying in class with an instructor, with tests and grades at the end. They learned about the many different systems used in spacecraft to keep humans alive in space. These include sophisticated flight controls, as well as air conditioning and other equipment. The trainees did some exercises on computers and others in life-size models of the craft itself.

LEARNING TO LIVE IN SPACE

Space travel can be tough on the body and the mind. Throughout training, astronauts have to prove they can survive these stresses. For example, they are exposed to very high and very low pressures in special sealed chambers.

They are also taught to operate in **weightless** conditions. This takes place in a big tank of water, which gives the same effect as the weightlessless felt in orbit. Each astronaut wears a **spacesuit**, which makes moving about even more difficult and exhausting.

■ Hadfield's training for his third space mission included more time underwater, to prepare him for weightless conditions.

SPACE AT LAST

On 12 November 1995, Chris Hadfield finally got to go to space. He made his first flight as an astronaut aboard a NASA space shuttle. The mission flew to the Russian space station *Mir*, where the crew fitted new parts and delivered supplies. Less than nine days later, they were back on Earth.

■ The space shuttle was carried to the edge of space by two rocket boosters and a huge tank of fuel.

SPACE Q AND A

Q. How do you build a space station?

A. The ISS is a huge structure – far too big to be launched into space in one piece. It was therefore carried to space in sections. The first section went into orbit in 1998. After that, 40 more missions were made to complete the space station. Altogether, the ISS took 12 years to be transported and constructed in space.

■ **Chris Hadfield worked on the ground as Capsule Communicator for 25 Shuttle missions.**

ON THE GROUND

Hadfield had a long wait before his second space flight. For the next six years he stayed on the ground, working in many roles. The most important was as Capsule Communicator (or **CAPCOM**). This is the person at NASA's Mission Control Center in Texas, USA, who has direct contact with the crews in orbit. In all, Hadfield was CAPCOM for 25 Shuttle missions.

BACK IN SPACE

Hadfield was also training for his second space mission. Finally, on 19 April 2001, he and six colleagues launched into space on the space shuttle *Endeavour*. The crew's destination was the brand new ISS.

Work on the ISS had begun just three years earlier, and it was still far from complete. The first crew had only arrived in 2000. Now Hadfield's crew were coming to help with the construction. Two days after launch, *Endeavour* **docked** with the space station.

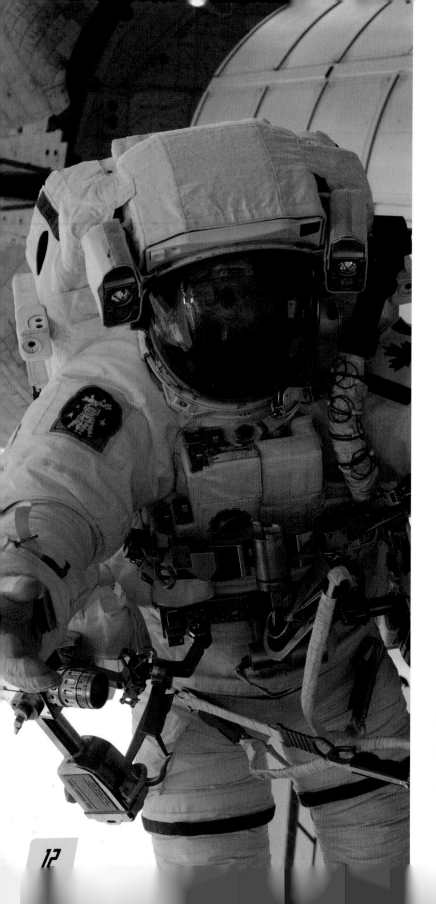

WORKING OUTSIDE

Two days later, Chris
Hadfield was ready
to leave *Endeavour*.
He was floating in the
airlock, wearing a
bulky spacesuit with
tools strapped to his
chest. On his back
were oxygen tanks for
breathing and a jet pack
for moving about.

Hadfield opened the
hatch and wriggled out
into space. He was in
Endeavour's loading
bay. He attached the
safety line on his suit
to a wire running the
length of the Shuttle.
This would stop him
floating away into space.
Then he waited for his
companion to join him.

■ Once outside, Chris
Hadfield lowered a gold
shield on his helmet to
protect his eyes from the
glare of the Sun.

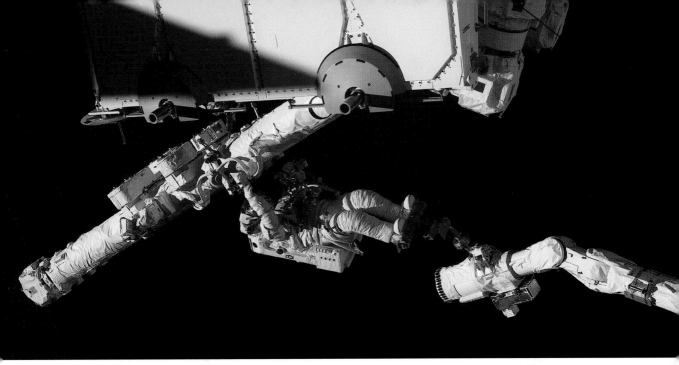

■ Hadfield stood on one robotic arm (right) in order to fix a second arm (left) to the Space Station.

USING THE ROBOT ARM

The main purpose of the mission was to install a huge **robotic arm**, called Canadarm2, on the outside of the ISS. It would be used to move supplies and catch (recover) satellites from orbit. Even more important, it would help to build the rest of the space station.

The **spacewalk** took over seven hours. The two astronauts worked steadily, tethered to the side of a Shuttle that was moving around Earth at 28,000 kilometres (17,500 miles) per hour. At last they completed the difficult job and returned to the Shuttle.

Going blind in space

Imagine you're floating in space. Your eyes begin to sting. You can't rub them because you've got a helmet on. Soon, they close up altogether and you can't see. This is exactly what happened to Chris Hadfield on his first spacewalk. Should he give up and stop what he was doing? No. Instead he waited, and soon his eyes began to clear. They'd been affected by a chemical he'd wiped on the inside of his helmet to keep the glass from misting up!

Focus on:

THE INTERNATIONAL SPACE STATION

MAIN PARTS OF THE ISS

The ISS is the largest spacecraft ever built. It covers an area about the size of a football field. The station is a framework of **trusses**, onto which cylinders and tubes are fixed. These are the **modules**, where the astronauts live and work. On top, looking like sails, are the huge solar panels that produce the station's power using the Sun's rays.

Facts and figures

The ISS has:

- 52 computers, which control the onboard systems
- 13 km (8 miles) of electrical wiring
- eight arrays of solar panels to generate electricity, covering 10,360 square kilometres (4,000 square miles)
- two bathrooms
- six sleeping stations (bedrooms)
- one robot arm crane, able to move objects as big as a space shuttle.

1 *Zarya:* the first module to be launched. It contained the power and guidance systems during the early years of construction, but is now used for storage.

2 *Zvezda:* contains most of the ISS's important electronic systems

3 *Destiny:* houses the station's US research facilities

4 *Quest:* when astronauts spacewalk, they exit through this airlock

5 *Columbus:* the area for European scientific research projects

6 *Kibo:* the main laboratory and the biggest module of all

7 docking ports: *Soyuz* and other spacecraft dock here

8 space vehicles: there is always at least one *Soyuz* at the station. The other craft to visit is the unmanned **Progress Supply Ship.**

9 main truss: major frame that holds the solar panels to the rest of the station

10 robot arm: moves along the main truss, carrying supplies or scientific equipment

11 cupola: the crew can view Earth through this large window

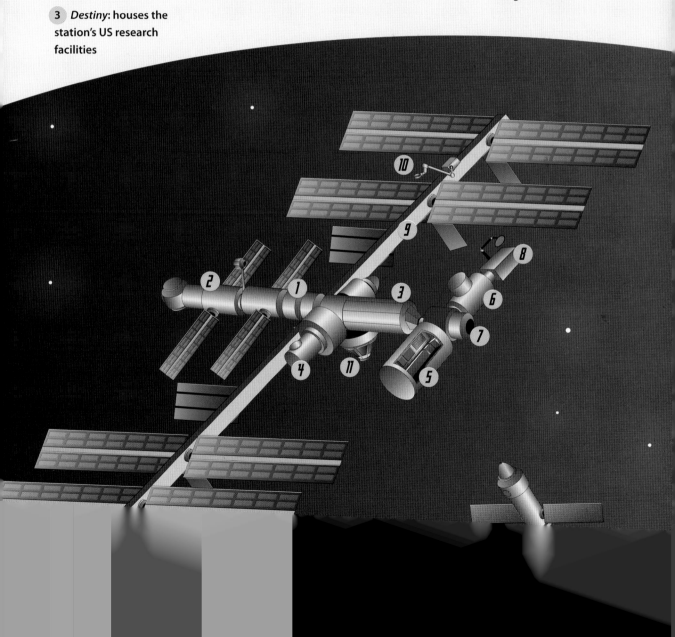

TRAINING FOR THE THIRD SPACE MISSION

Mission accomplished, Chris Hadfield and the *Endeavour* returned to Earth after 11 days. He was still an astronaut, but he wondered if he would ever return to space.

LIFE IN RUSSIA

Hadfield didn't worry about spending time on the ground. He was happy to learn new skills and gain different experiences. Soon after his 2001 flight, NASA sent him to be director of their operations in Russia. The United States and Russia were working together on developing the ISS. Hadfield was based in Star City, near Moscow, the centre for space training and research in Russia.

Hadfield's main job in Star City was to help with the selection and training of space station crew members, but he also learned to fly the Russian *Soyuz* spacecraft. In order to do this, he had to become fluent in Russian.

SPACE SPEAK

Astronaut or cosmonaut?
Space crew from the United States or Great Britain are called "astronauts" (from the Greek meaning "star sailor"). Russian space crew are usually called "cosmonauts" (from the Greek meaning "space traveller").

ANOTHER SPACE MISSION

Hadfield returned to the United States in 2003, to work in the Houston Space Center, Texas. Then, in 2010, he at last received the news that he would be returning to the ISS. This time, he would lead the expedition.

For the next two years, Hadfield trained for the new mission. The biggest change was the vehicle; the space shuttle programme had ended, so Hadfield and his crew would be travelling to the ISS in a *Soyuz*, launching from Russia.

■ **Hadfield (left) trained for his next mission by spending time in an underwater habitat.**

TAKE-OFF

On 19 December 2012, 11 years after his last mission, Chris Hadfield sat wedged in his seat on the *Soyuz* spacecraft. The craft sat on top of a gigantic rocket on a launch site in Kazakhstan, near the border with Russia. Beside him were American Tom Marshburn and Russian Roman Romanenko. The three men had been sitting there for more than two hours, checking the controls and safety systems.

Thirty seconds before launch, Hadfield felt a rumbling beneath him. The massive rocket engines had been fired. The noise grew as he listened to the countdown to zero through his headphones. Then came the word "Lift-off", and the rocket rose into the sky.

After two minutes, the *Soyuz* was already 40 kilometres (25 miles) away from Earth's surface. The **first-stage rockets** cut out and exploded off the side. The craft suddenly picked up speed as it became lighter. Hadfield was slammed back into his seat by the extra force.

OUT OF THE ATMOSPHERE

The same thing happened when the second-stage engines whizzed away from the *Soyuz*, and the third-stage engines fired. They were now 240 kilometres (150 miles) above Earth. Only nine minutes from launch, the third stage was gone too.

Soon the spacecraft was out of Earth's **atmosphere**. Its solar panels were unfolded and it flew into orbit, powered by energy from the Sun. The crew were free of the pull of **gravity**. They could take off their bulky spacesuits and relax a little.

■ The *Soyuz* lifts off from its launchpad at Baikonur cosmodrone.

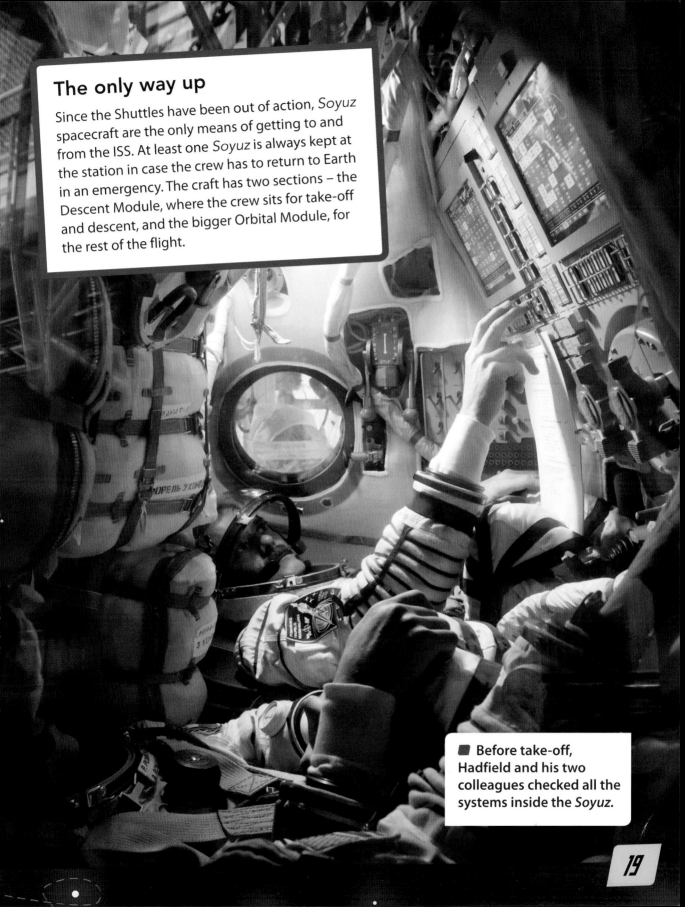

The only way up

Since the Shuttles have been out of action, *Soyuz* spacecraft are the only means of getting to and from the ISS. At least one *Soyuz* is always kept at the station in case the crew has to return to Earth in an emergency. The craft has two sections – the Descent Module, where the crew sits for take-off and descent, and the bigger Orbital Module, for the rest of the flight.

◾ Before take-off, Hadfield and his two colleagues checked all the systems inside the *Soyuz*.

A NEW HOME

Once the *Soyuz* was in space, and had climbed into the same orbit as the ISS, Hadfield was able to see the space station in the distance, shining like a star.

DOCKING

Two days after launch, the *Soyuz* bumped gently into the docking bay of the ISS. The crews connected the craft with the ISS and checked the seals between the hatches were not damaged. Any leak would lower the **air pressure** inside the space station and put lives in danger.

When all was safe, they opened the hatch and floated into the ISS. They were greeted by the astronauts already on board – two Russians and one American. Next, for the first time since the launch, they spoke to their families through a television link to the mission control centre in Kazakhstan.

■ This photograph of the *Soyuz* spacecraft approaching the ISS was taken by one of the ISS crew members.

Sticky walls

Everything floats in space, because in orbit objects are weightless. That's why many of the ISS's walls are covered in Velcro, and small items, such as pens, cutlery and tools, have Velcro patches. This allows the crew to "stick" the small items to the walls when they're not using them!

TAKING COMMAND

When Hadfield first flew to the ISS in 2001, he never went on board. This time, he was going to be living on the station for five months. What's more, he would be its commander – the first Canadian to take the post.

On 13 March 2013, the previous station boss, US astronaut Kevin Ford, officially handed over command. He even played the Canadian national anthem for Hadfield. After this, Ford and his two Russian colleagues headed back to Earth. Three new arrivals on the ISS replaced them two weeks later.

■ **When they entered the ISS, Hadfield (left) and Marshburn (middle) were greeted by Expedition Commander Kevin Ford (right).**

WHAT IS LIFE LIKE ON THE ISS?

The ISS isn't like an ordinary home or office. It's full of long, narrow passages, with other passages going off sideways, up and down. There are no windows, and the only place for a good outside view is the cupola (see pages 15 and 26).

GETTING USED TO IT

Chris Hadfield already knew most of the layout aboard the ISS, since he had studied a computer 3D model of the station on Earth. Having been in space before, he was also used to living in cramped conditions. On the ISS, most modules are so narrow that Hadfield could almost touch both sides with outstretched arms.

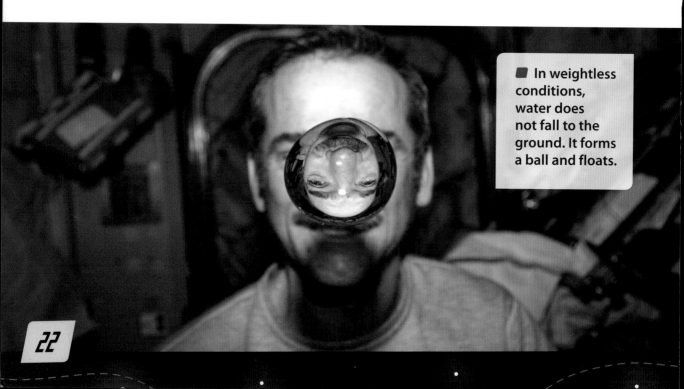

■ In weightless conditions, water does not fall to the ground. It forms a ball and floats.

He also had to get used to the constant noises. In low gravity, air does not move about. To keep it fresh, fans and pumps whirred away, mixing warm and cool air. Other system machines added their own hums and clunks.

KEEPING FIT

A station crew lives in weightless conditions for many weeks. This can have a bad effect on the body. Without the effort of overcoming the drag of gravity, muscles and bones will waste away. So each astronaut has to exercise for at least two hours every day to keep fit and strong. The station has specially adapted equipment, including a **treadmill** (for running), a stationary bike and weights (for lifting).

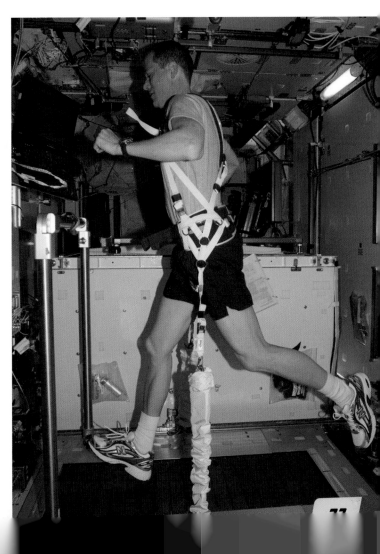

■ This flight engineer is exercising on a treadmill on board the ISS.

Danger: meteorites!

Another noise astronauts report is the ping of tiny objects hitting the outside of the ISS. These are either pieces of space junk that are still in orbit, or very small **meteorites** (rocky lumps that fly through space).The station is covered in armour to protect it. But this would be useless against a really big meteorite, which could cause serious damage.

LEARNING TO FLOAT

Being weightless in a large spaceship is a lot of fun. Hadfield found he was able to move about by simply pushing off a wall and floating through the air, or flying down the passages. Lifting huge objects is easy, because they weigh almost nothing.

BED AND BATHROOM

But weightlessness also creates problems. How do you brush your teeth when the water and toothpaste will simply drift away? Hadfield learned to wash his hands in a bag of water and always swallow his toothpaste. Going to the toilet is also tricky. Suction hoses take away waste matter, and the crew have to be very careful not to spill anything!

Finally, astronauts go to bed in their tiny private chambers. They zip themselves into a sleeping bag, which is connected to the wall. In space, there's no need for a pillow or a mattress. As Hadfield says, it's like "resting on a cloud".

■ Astronauts in the ISS can sleep anywhere – on the floor, walls or even the ceiling.

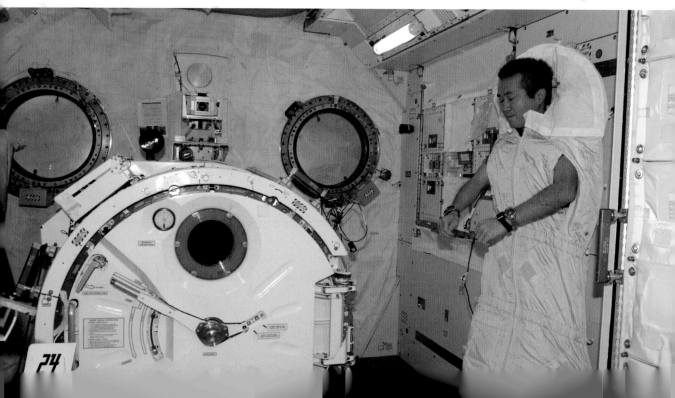

SPACE Q AND A

Q. What happens to sweat in space?

A. Exercise makes us sweat. In space, sweat doesn't drip off like it does on Earth. Instead, it gathers on your body. When you move, a ball of liquid might fly off and hit someone else. Astronauts always carry a towel to soak up their sweat. The moisture, like that in urine, is then cleaned and recycled as drinking water.

FLOATING FOOD

Astronauts often add water to different types of dried food and drink in bags. The food has to be contained in a bag or tin, or it will float away and cause damage.

SIXTEEN SUNSETS A DAY!

The cupola is a domed window on the bottom of the ISS. From here, astronauts have an amazing view of Earth. The view changes all the time, as Earth spins past and the station flies on its orbit.

The ISS moves at an average speed of more than 27,000 kilometres (17,000 miles) per hour. This means it travels round Earth nearly 16 times a day, moving west to east, into the sunrise. The crew gets to see the Sun rise and set every 92 minutes.

■ **This photograph shows part of Australia as the ISS passes over it. Several of the ISS's solar panels can also be seen.**

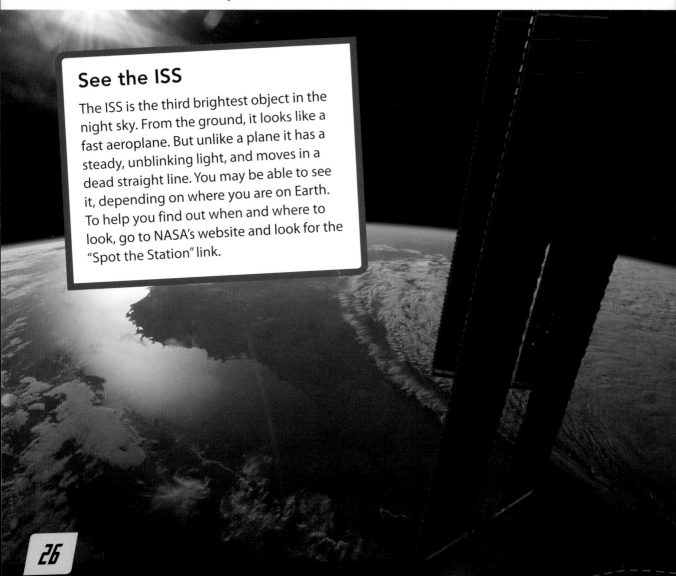

See the ISS
The ISS is the third brightest object in the night sky. From the ground, it looks like a fast aeroplane. But unlike a plane it has a steady, unblinking light, and moves in a dead straight line. You may be able to see it, depending on where you are on Earth. To help you find out when and where to look, go to NASA's website and look for the "Spot the Station" link.

■ This photograph of Vancouver, Canada, at night was taken by an ISS crew member.

LOOKING DOWN ON EARTH

Chris Hadfield was astonished by the beauty of the world below, with its endless variety of colours and shapes. By day he could see familiar landmarks, such as seas, mountains, coastlines, deserts and rivers. Where it was night, he could see great cities light up. All around these sights was the pitch blackness of space.

Astronauts in the ISS also have unique views of extraordinary things on Earth. They see the flickering of the Northern Lights (a dramatic display of colours in the Arctic skies), the spiralling storm clouds of giant hurricanes over the Atlantic, and the brilliant glow of the moon rising over the Pacific.

WHAT WORK IS DONE ABOARD THE ISS?

What is the ISS for? After all, it has cost well over £80 billion to create, making it probably the most expensive object ever built. The ISS is actually a huge research platform up in space, where the astronauts carry out many kinds of experiments and collect data that could change our lives.

■ Hadfield monitored his own blood pressure as part of the medical experiments carried out on board.

IN THE LABORATORY

Every morning, Chris Hadfield and his crew received a list of tasks from Mission Control on Earth. Apart from checking the station systems and cleaning, the main jobs were in the laboratory modules.

They tested each other's hearts, blood and eye pressure to see how human bodies react to long periods in space. They studied plants to see how they grow in low gravity. Hadfield's favourite project involved a machine called a **spectrometer**, which collects particles and dark matter (see box). This research could help discover what the Universe is made of.

SUCCESS STORIES

Here are some of the top achievements of ISS research teams:

- Human health: a big advance in the treatment of cancer, using tiny doses of chemicals to treat patients. Asthma sufferers have been helped by the development of small devices that monitor the air they breathe.
- Water for everyone: technology used to recycle water on the ISS may be used to help deliver clean water to remote locations
- Inspiring young people: links with the station have fired the imaginations of students in many areas, from engineering to photography.

SPACE SPEAK

Dark matter: You can't see dark matter, even with a telescope. But scientists believe it makes up about 27 per cent of the Universe. They know there is something out there that behaves differently from the "normal" matter you can see, such as **planets** and stars.

INSPIRING PEOPLE FROM SPACE

Chris Hadfield had lots of work to do on board the ISS. Yet he still found time for something extra – telling the world about the space station, the NASA space programme and its achievements.

■ The video of Hadfield singing David Bowie's "Space Oddity" became a worldwide hit.

Hadfield began making videos about daily life on the ISS, from getting a haircut to exercising. These were posted on YouTube and became very popular.

He also spent a lot of free time in the cupola, from which he took photographs of Earth. He posted the best pictures on social media sites, to show people the beauty of space travel. Then he recorded the sounds inside the ISS and posted those as well. He soon had thousands of followers.

THE SINGING SPACEMAN

Hadfield had brought a guitar with him to space. He decided to take part in a live music broadcast, singing alongside nearly one million children all over the world. But he was about to become even more famous. In May 2013, he recorded a version of David Bowie's classic song "Space Oddity" and posted it to YouTube. Within a few weeks, the video had received over 7 million hits.

SPACE Q AND A

Q. Are rockets and space stations worth the expense?

A. Some think the space programme is a waste of money. They believe the money would be better spent on other things, such as helping hungry or sick people on Earth. On the other hand, the space programme aims to do something amazing – explore our part of the Universe and help us to understand space. Do you think that's worth the money – or not?

■ **Hadfield posted photographs of himself and the rest of the crew celebrating Christmas on the ISS.**

Focus on:

DANGERS IN SPACE

Flying into space is one of the most dangerous things humans can do. It's a hostile environment, which can kill you in a few seconds if you have no protection. It's also a very hard place to get rescued from in an emergency. Astronauts know that death is never too far away. To survive, they have to remember their training and think clearly.

WHAT ARE THE BIGGEST THREATS IN SPACE?

Here are some of the major hazards facing crew members on the ISS:

- Take-off: The launch is the riskiest moment of all. The astronauts are strapped on top of a giant rocket packed with highly explosive fuel. Many complicated systems all have to operate perfectly. One small failure could cause disaster.

- Fire: Flames are much harder to put out in weightless conditions, and spread in all directions. You can't run away from a burning spacecraft.

- Losing pressure: There is no air pressure in space. The air inside spaceships and spacesuits is kept at the same pressure as on Earth. Without pressure, the fluids in your body would boil, then freeze. A leak would cause a quick death.

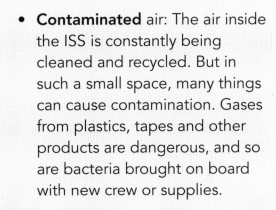

- **Contaminated** air: The air inside the ISS is constantly being cleaned and recycled. But in such a small space, many things can cause contamination. Gases from plastics, tapes and other products are dangerous, and so are bacteria brought on board with new crew or supplies.

Mission Control

Large teams of flight controllers at two Mission Controls operated by Russia and the United States, keep a constant watch on every aspect of life on the ISS. This includes monitoring air quality and other possible threats to safety. In an emergency, the controllers give advice and guidance.

RETURNING TO EARTH

Four days before Hadfield was due to come home, a crew member saw sparks flying from the left side of the station. Had they been hit by a meteorite? They took photographs of the mysterious flashes and sent them to Mission Control.

EMERGENCY!

Soon a message came back: the flashes were caused by **ammonia** leaking into space. This was serious. Ammonia is used to cool the station's huge batteries and other power systems. Without it, these would have to be switched off so they didn't overheat.

Worse still, the leak was growing. It needed to be fixed, and fast. Two crew members would have to go into space to make repairs. Usually astronauts need at least a week to prepare for a spacewalk. Now they had just one day.

SPACE Q AND A

Q. What happens in a major emergency?

A. Astronauts are trained to solve any problem on board. But what if the emergency is so bad it cannot be fixed, and the lives of the crew are at risk? They would have to fly back to Earth in the *Soyuz* craft docked to the station. If the ISS survived, its systems could still be operated from Mission Control.

URGENT REPAIRS

The crew tested the equipment, then worked out each move in the repair sequence. The next morning, Hadfield helped his two US colleagues into their spacesuits, then into the airlock. As commander, he stayed on board to direct the operation.

The spacewalkers climbed out to replace the ammonia pump. It took over five hours, and both men were exhausted when they returned to the safety of the ISS. But they'd stopped the leak. The danger was over.

■ **Two US astronauts went outside the Space Station to fix a leaking pump.**

PACKING UP

It was nearly time to go back to Earth. The day after the emergency spacewalk, Hadfield officially handed over command of the ISS to Russian astronaut Pavel Vinogradov. Then he and his two crewmates, Romanenko and Marshburn, began the final preparations.

One of the most crucial tasks was to pack equipment into the *Soyuz*. In such a small space, everything had to be in exactly the right position. The spacecraft had to be perfectly balanced so it would fly straight. The only person allowed to do this was Romanenko, who had been specially trained for this task.

Meanwhile, Hadfield and Marshburn tidied up their module and gathered their belongings. They shot last-minute videos for family and friends back home. More importantly, they practised the landing procedures, using a simulation programme on a computer.

SPACE Q AND A

Q. Where does the rubbish go?

A. Rubbish from the space station is loaded into the Orbital Module of the *Soyuz*. During the descent towards Earth, this part of the craft detaches from the Descent Module. Without a pilot or any protection, it burns up when it re-enters the atmosphere.

READY TO DESCEND

On 13 May 2013, the three astronauts climbed back into their little spacecraft. The Descent Module was already crammed with their personal belongings, as well as samples from scientific experiments. They checked the pressure and other controls, and pulled on their spacesuits. Then the *Soyuz* was released from the docking port. It fired its thrusters and moved away from the ISS and into space.

◼ Hadfield's *Soyuz* craft undocked from the ISS at the start of its journey back to Earth.

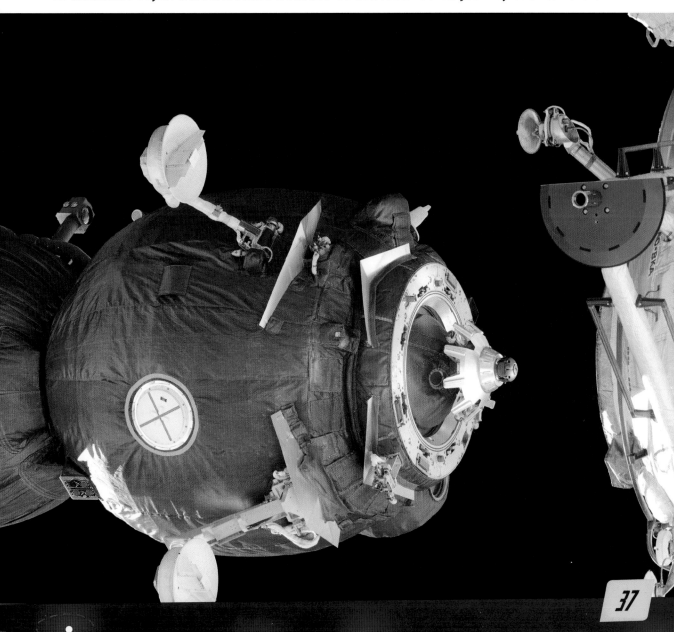

HEADING FOR EARTH

Soon the *Soyuz* was a safe distance from the ISS. The engines were fired for a few seconds, to push the craft into a lower orbit. Two and a half hours later, the engines were started again. This took the spacecraft to the edge of the atmosphere, and the start of the long, tumbling spin towards Earth.

HITTING THE GROUND

The air in Earth's atmosphere is denser than in space. This causes drag, which slowed down the *Soyuz*. It also creates a lot of heat. Hadfield saw flames and sparks flying off the spacecraft. But it was protected from burning by a thick layer called the **ablative shield** (see box).

When they finally opened the parachutes, the craft suddenly stopped spinning and slowed more. Even so, the impact on the ground was heavy. The three men were dazed and exhausted, but they were alive.

■ Slowed by the parachute, the *Soyuz* headed to land at a speed of 1.5 metres (5 feet) per second.

BACK HOME

The astronauts landed back in Kazakhstan. Russian ground crews opened the door to the *Soyuz* and helped them out. The crew were taken straight to medical staff to be checked and rested. After five months of weightlessness, the astronauts' bodies were very weak.

Hadfield didn't get home for another day. When he arrived in Texas, he finally got to see his wife and family – and enjoy a proper shower. And then he had a very long sleep.

◼ After leaving the spacecraft, the crew rested in chairs before being checked by medical staff.

SPACE SPEAK

Ablative shield: The *Soyuz* heat shield looks just like a giant saucer fitted to the bottom of the Descent Module. It's made of special "ablative" material, which protects the craft against burning up. The material "ablates", or burns very slowly, and breaks off in small pieces. This carries heat away from the craft.

Focus on:

TRAVELLING TO MARS

■ Two Rover vehicles landed on Mars in January 2004.

The ISS is very near Earth. The Moon is much farther away but is our nearest neighbour in space. Since we landed there nearly 50 years ago, space engineers have been planning to send a mission to one of our nearest neighbours – the planet Mars. Will they succeed?

THE RED PLANET

Mars is about half the size of Earth. Its surface is covered in dust and rocks that are rich in iron. This makes it look red. You can easily spot the "Red Planet" from Earth with the naked eye. But Mars is a hostile place.

- It's very cold. The average temperature is -60 degrees Celsius (-80 degrees Fahrenheit).
- We can't breathe the air because it's 95 per cent carbon dioxide, with very little oxygen.
- The air also has only 1 percent as much pressure as on Earth. The human body would explode if not protected.
- While ice has been found on Mars, there is no evidence of any liquid water.
- Huge dust storms often cover the entire surface and can last for months.

GETTING THERE

There are now two robot vehicles, *Opportunity* and *Curiosity*, exploring Mars. The next test is to get humans there.

One important purpose for a new space station would be as a command centre for exploring Mars. Flying astronauts directly to other planets is costly and dangerous. It's much cheaper and safer to travel from a space station in orbit above the planet. But a human landing on Mars is still a long way off – NASA plans to send astronauts there during the 2030s. Could you be one of them?

How far away from Earth?	Distance	Flying time
International Space Station	400 km (250 miles)	6 hours
Moon	380,000 km (240,000 miles)	3 days
Mars	228,000,000 km (140,000,000 miles)	8 months

THE FUTURE FOR HADFIELD AND THE ISS

Chris Hadfield spent more time in space than most other astronauts. After his spell as commander of the ISS in 2013, he decided to retire from NASA. But he continued to teach people about the achievements of the space programme and wrote a best-selling book, *An Astronaut's Guide to Life on Earth*.

■ **Chris Hadfield toured the world telling people about the NASA space programme.**

THE FUTURE OF THE ISS

The ISS is still travelling around Earth. How long will it last? Right now, the partner countries plan to keep it going until 2024, and some of its equipment until 2028. When its work comes to an end, it will probably be brought back into Earth's atmosphere and splashed down in the Pacific Ocean, nearly 30 years after it was first launched.

TOMORROW'S SPACE STATIONS

The ISS has helped us to discover a lot about living and working in space. But what kind of space stations may be built in years to come?

- Factories for assembling big spacecraft (much easier to do in low gravity)
- Repair plants for servicing satellites
- Petrol stations for fuelling long-distance spacecraft
- Hotels for space tourists

ROBOT PIONEERS

Robots could be sent ahead to the Moon or Mars to construct buildings and other important installations. Perhaps they could be sent to explore distant and dangerous places in space. They may even land on **asteroids**!

Spaceships of the future

As humans build space stations further from home, new craft will be needed to shuttle astronauts to and from Earth. Many ideas are dreamt up, such as the British "Spacecab", which holds eight people. Others, like the Japanese "Kankoh-Maru", could carry up to 50 passengers. However, it remains to be seen whether anything like these ideas will ever be built.

TIMELINE

19 August 1959	Chris Hadfield is born in Ontario, Canada
20 July 1969	*Apollo 11* lands the first humans on the Moon
1978	Hadfield joins the Canadian Armed Forces
1983	Hadfield is the top graduate from the Basic Jet Pilot course in Canada
1988	Hadfield joins Test Pilot School in California, USA
June 1992	Hadfield is selected to train as one of four Canadian astronauts in Texas, USA
12–20 November 1995	Hadfield's first launch into space, aboard space shuttle *Atlantis*. The Shuttle docks with the Russian space station *Mir*.
1996	Hadfield covers 25 Shuttle missions from the ground as Capsule Communicator (CAPCOM)
1998	Construction of the International Space Station (ISS) begins
19 April–1 May 2001	Hadfield's second Shuttle flight docks with the ISS. He becomes the first Canadian to walk in space.
	Hadfield becomes NASA's Director of Operations in Star City, Moscow, Russia
2003	Hadfield returns to NASA HQ at Houston, Texas, USA
2010	Hadfield is appointed Commander of Expedition 35 to the ISS
19 December 2012	Hadfield takes off for the ISS aboard a *Soyuz* spacecraft
14 March 2013	Hadfield officially takes command of the ISS
13 May 2013	Hadfield returns to Earth. His autobiography is published later the same year.
2014	Hadfield is appointed officer of the Order of Canada, in recognition of his achievements

GLOSSARY

ablative shield shield that protects a spacecraft from heat by melting or flaking

airlock airtight chamber between two areas of unequal air pressure

air pressure force exerted on our bodies by the weight of the air above, caused by the pull of gravity

ammonia colourless and strong-smelling gas

applicant person who applies for a job or post

asteroid rocky bodies of rock and iron that orbit the Sun

astronaut person trained to travel into space aboard a spacecraft

atmosphere protective layer of air and other gases that surrounds the planet, allowing living things to survive

CAPCOM short for Capsule Communicator, the person at NASA's Mission Control Center in Texas, USA, who has direct contact with the crews in orbit

contaminated when something has become harmful or poisonous because unsafe substances have been added to it

cupola dome-shaped ceiling or window

dock process of attaching one spacecraft to another

first-stage rockets rocket engines that carry a spacecraft off the launch pad. These are then dumped and the second-stage engines take over.

gravity pulling force that attracts objects to one another and prevents weightlessness

hatch opening or doorway in a spacecraft

meteorite fragment of rock orbiting the Sun which has hit a spacecraft or landed on a planet

module one of the living or working units that make up a spacecraft

orbit curved path an object follows around a planet, or other celestial body, as a result of its gravity

planet huge ball of rock, gas or ice, that orbits another, bigger object

Progress supply ship Russian spacecraft that carries food and other supplies to space stations. It has no pilot, and is allowed to burn up as it re-enters Earth's atmosphere.

research laboratory specially equipped area where scientific experiments are carried out

robotic arm space crane, operated from inside the ISS, used to construct or repair the station, or capture satellites and other objects

satellite object that orbits a star, planet or asteroid. Satellites can be natural, such as the Moon, or man-made, such as *Sputnik 1*.

smoke detector device that sets off a fire alarm when it senses smoke

spacesuit suit that protects astronauts from the hostile conditions in space (including very low pressure and lack of oxygen)

spacewalk to go outside a spacecraft, usually to work on repairs to the spacecraft or a satellite

spectrometer instrument that takes in light and breaks it up into its different colours so they can be examined

test pilot pilot who tries out new and experimental versions of aircraft

treadmill machine with a moving belt, used for running or walking in one place

truss metal framework that supports or holds together parts of a building or machine

weightless something that is weightless is held down by gravity. In space, the force of gravity is not felt.

FIND OUT MORE

BOOKS

Astronaut: Living in Space (DK Readers: Level 2), Deborah Lock; Kate Hayden (Dorling Kindersley, 2013)

Chris Hadfield (Canadian Biographies), Chelsea Donaldson (Capstone, 2014)

Space: A Children's Encyclopedia (Dorling Kindersley, 2010)

Space Exploration (Space Travel Guides), Giles Sparrow (Franklin Watts, 2013)

DVDs

Chris Hadfield: The Man Who Tweeted Earth (2013)
This is a record of Chris Hadfield's amazing stay in space.

Into the Void – The International Space Station (2010)
This is three documentary films covering the history of the ISS.

WEBSITES

www.nasa.gov/audience/forstudents
This is a younger reader's website run by the US space agency.

www.nasa.gov/mission_pages/station/main/
The official NASA site has live pictures and lots of information about space.

www.spacesafetymagazine.com/*Soyuz*-launch-sequence-explained/
Check out this website to see animation of the full sequence of *Soyuz* launch and getting into orbit.

spacestationlive.nasa.gov/displays/evaDisplay1.html
Be a flight controller! Watch the screen displays in NASA Mission Control.

www.theatlantic.com/infocus/2014/05/viewing-the-earth-from-space/100740/
This website has some amazing images of Earth photographed from the ISS.

www.youtube.com/watch?v=doN4t5NKW-k
See a video of astronaut Sunita Williams giving a conducted tour of the ISS.

HOW CAN I FIND OUT MORE?

Our exploration of space is a topic as big as the universe itself. Here are some ideas for your research:

- Spaceships of the future: What will they look like? How will they be powered? Find out about technology that is being developed to power new spacecraft.

- Going beyond the Solar System: Which spacecraft has gone the farthest? The answer is the US *Voyager 1*, heading into outer space since 1977!

- The Rosetta comet mission: The European Space Agency succeeded in landing a craft on the surface of a comet. See if you can find out what information the craft, called *Philae*, has sent back to Earth.

- Looking for aliens: Is there anyone else out there? As far as we know, life only exists on Earth. But somewhere in one of the billions of other galaxies something else may be alive.

INDEX